Seven Steps to Forgiveness with Jesus

For Youth Groups, Jesus Lovers, Church Leaders, Bible Study Groups, and Families eager for a deeper understanding of our Lord Jesus Christ

(Study Guide Included)

Debbie Dunn

FYI - Unless otherwise noted, most Biblical quotes come from either the King James Version (KJV) or the New International Version (NIV) of the Bible APP.

Permissions: This book or any portion thereof may not be reproduced or used in any manner without the publisher's express written permission except for using brief quotations in a book review. For copy permission, please email the author, Debbie Dunn, at moredunntales@yahoo.com. Place, in the subject line: **Seven Steps to Forgiveness with Jesus**

Disclaimer: The content used in this book is intended for educational and informational purposes only.

Imprint: Independently published. Distributed by Draft 2 Digital
ISBN: 9798227850577

T.R.E.A.T. Tales Presents

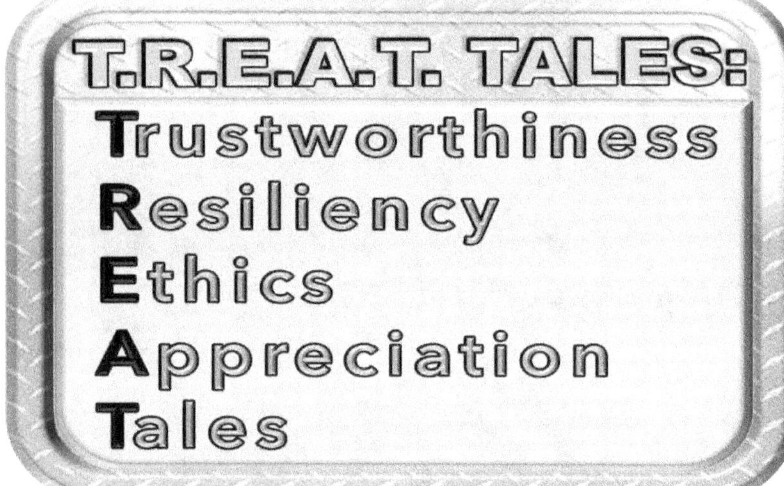

FYI - Fifty percent (50%) of all book sales will be donated to **covenanthouse.org** to *"join the fight to end youth homelessness."*

Website: https://bible-books-for-his-glory.com/index.html
Email: moredunntales@yahoo.com

About the Author: Debbie Dunn

Debbie Dunn has been a professional storyteller since 1989. She has also taught at-risk teens, served as an anti-bullying specialist, and taught elementary and middle school. In her retirement years, she indulges her love of our Lord Jesus Christ, nature, traveling, and writing as she pursues learning and exploring more about the Holy Bible.

Table of Contents

About the Book

In **Matthew 5:21-24** and **Matthew 7:1-5,** Jesus gave us two directives about forgiveness and leaving judgment of others to Almighty God. How do we go about doing that? This book describes a 7-step process as one of the many methods that might work for you when forgiving others. If we want to be covered by the Holy Blood of Jesus and see our name written in the Lamb's Book of Life, we must let go of all grudges against others.

Some of the points this book covers include:
* Righteous Indignation versus Wrath
* 12 free resources in cases of Domestic Violence and other types of abuse
* Exploring what might happen if you refuse to forgive
* Judgment Day: Bema seat versus Great White Throne
* Judgment Day Thought Experiment for both Believers and non-believers facing Christ
* Judgment Day: 5 crowns earned by Believers
* Verbal Abuse Examples
* How to break the Grudge-holding Habit
* The Six Responses to Trauma: 5 Fs plus Jesus
* Putting on the Armor of God

Seven Steps to Forgiveness with Jesus is a book specifically crafted for youth groups, Jesus lovers, church leaders, Bible study groups, and families who are eager for a deeper understanding of our Lord Jesus Christ. The author, understanding the unique needs of these groups, has filled this book with conceptual illustrations that will resonate with them, and has included a study guide for their convenience.

Fifty percent (50%) of all book sales will be donated to **Covenant House** to "***join the fight to end youth homelessness.***"

FYI – This is a stand-alone book pulled from four sections of my 75-chapter book titled, "Jesus' Crucifixion and Resurrection foretold by 12 Biblical Prophets & Kings." Those four sections include:

Seven Steps to Forgiveness with Jesus	*Jesus' Crucifixion and Resurrection ... Book*
Chapter 1 of this book is the same as	*Chapter 71 of my other book.*
Study Guide for Chapter 1 is same as	*Study Guide for Chapter 71 of my other book.*
Chapter 2 is the same as	*Chapter 74 of my other book.*
Chapter 3 is a shortened Bibliography	*found in Chapter 75 of my other book.*

SEVEN STEPS TO FORGIVENESS WITH JESUS

To begin, please consider these two directives from Jesus about forgiveness.

Matthew 7:1 "Do not judge, or you too will be judged. **2** For in the same way you judge others, you will be judged, and with the measure you use, it will be measured to you.

Matthew 7:3 Why do you look at the speck of sawdust in your brother's eye and pay no attention to the plank in your own eye?

Matthew 7:4 How can you say to your brother, 'Let me take the speck out of your eye,' when all the time there is a plank in your own eye?

Matthew 7:5 You hypocrite, first take the plank out of your own eye, and then you will see clearly to remove the speck from your brother's eye."

Matthew 5:21 You have heard that it was said to the people long ago, 'You shall not murder, and anyone who murders will be subject to judgment.'

Matthew 5:22 But I tell you that anyone who is angry with a brother or sister will be subject to judgment. Again, anyone who says to a brother or sister, 'Raca,' is answerable to the court. And anyone who says, 'You fool!' will be in danger of the fire of hell."

GOOGLE QUOTE: "The word 'Raca' means a worthless, empty-headed man; a brainless idiot, foolish, witless."

GOOGLE QUOTE: "In the Bible a fool is one who has rebelled against God. When we call someone a fool as a sign of our hatred towards them, then it's sinful. But saying someone is being foolish because they're rebelling against God, and it's true, we've did them a favor. The word "fool" doesn't signify a person that's ignorant."

Matthew 5:23 "Therefore, if you are offering your gift at the altar and there remember that your brother or sister has something against you, **24** leave your gift there in front of the altar. First go and be reconciled to them; then come and offer your gift." (NIV)

The following 7-step process is one of many methods that might work for you when forgiving others.

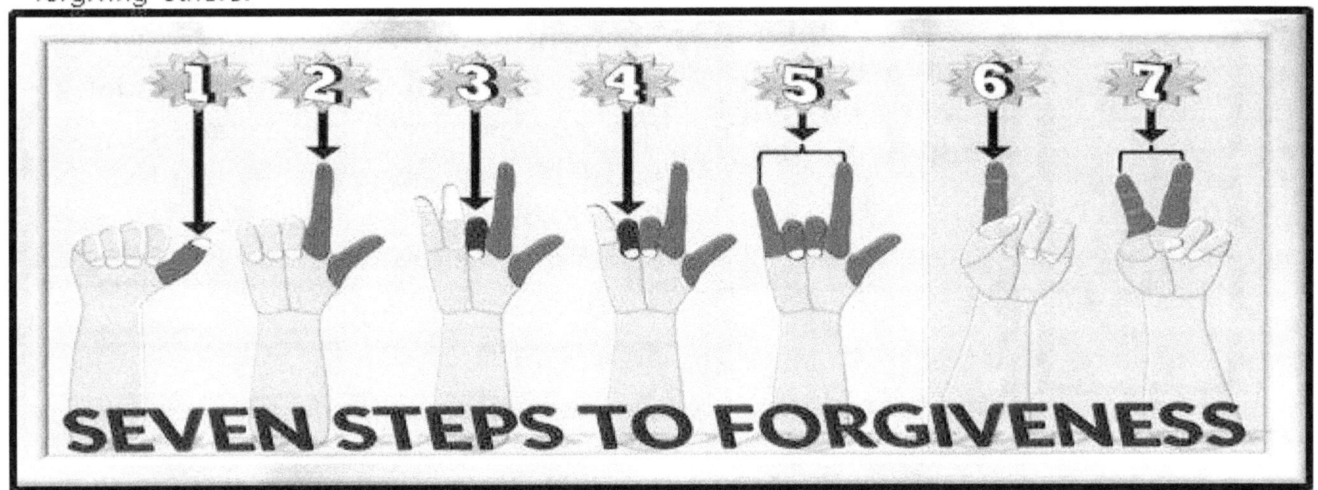

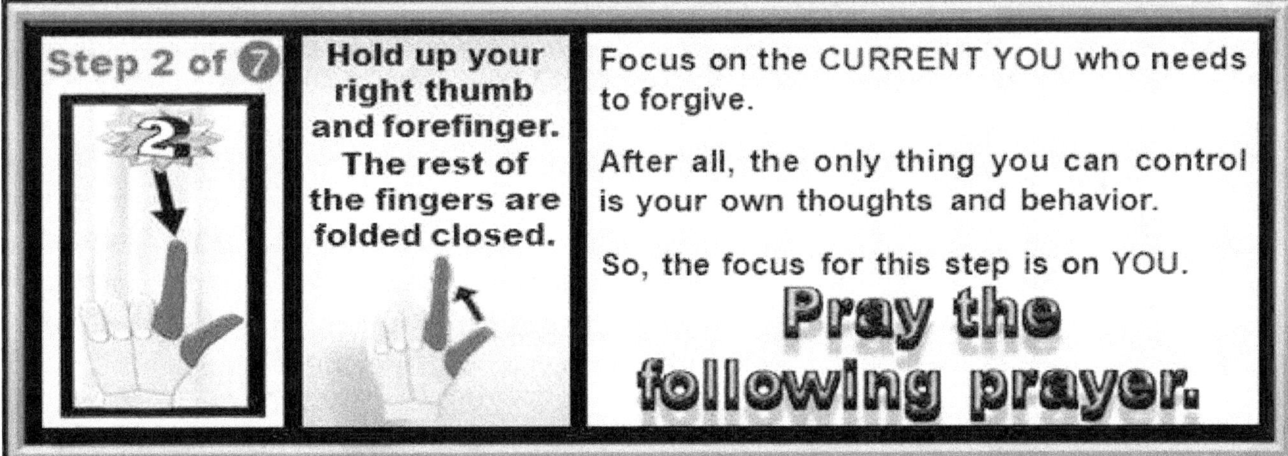

"Dear God, I am aware of Your directive in the Lord's Prayer that if I wish for You to forgive me, I must forgive others. Please give me the strength, moral courage, and ability to forgive this person (or situation) in Jesus' Holy name."

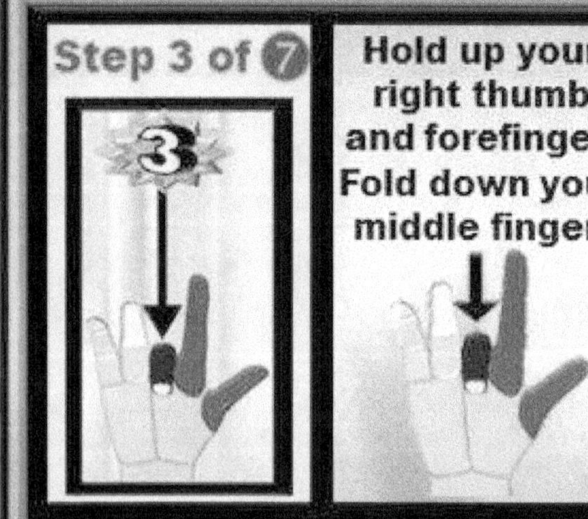

CURRENT YOU must forgive PAST YOU (whether it happened 5 minutes ago or 5 years ago, etc.) for not handling things as well as you could have.

"CURRENT ME forgives PAST ME for not handling things as well as I could have at that time. This is what I now understand (or realize)":

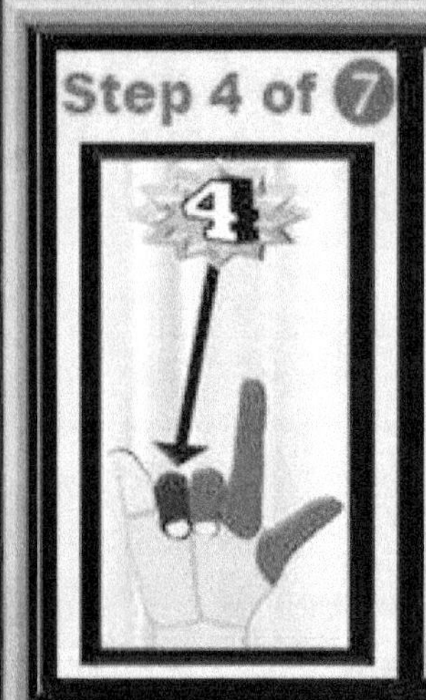
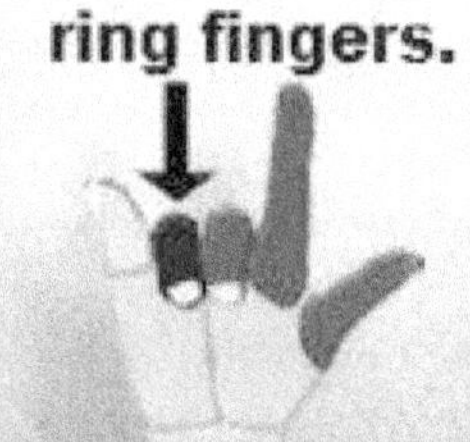

CURRENT YOU must forgive PAST THEM (or PAST IT if it is a situation).

"CURRENT ME forgives PAST THEM (or PAST IT if it is a situation). I forgive the person you were on that day. Knowing what we know now, we probably could have handled things better. This is what I now understand (or realize)":

CURRENT YOU must forgive CURRENT THEM (or CURRENT IT if it is a situation).

With that 'I love you' hand signal, send Agape Love (Loving as Christ Loves, with a capital L) to that person or situation. **Pray the following prayer.**

"CURRENT ME forgives CURRENT THEM (or CURRENT IT if it is a situation). I forgive you and send you Agape Love (of Christ). I thank you for giving me this opportunity to learn some important lessons."

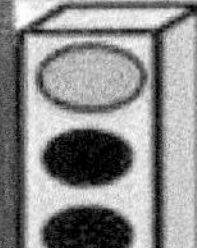

If you no longer want them in your life:

"Even though I no longer want you to be part of my life, I still wish all the best for you now and in the future."

"Also, I would like to communicate the following to you, in person or only in my thoughts: _______________________________________
____."

If you still want them as part of your life:

"I definitely want you to continue to be a part of my life. I wish all the best for you now and in your future."

"Also, I would like to communicate the following to you, in person or only in my thoughts: _______________________________________
____."

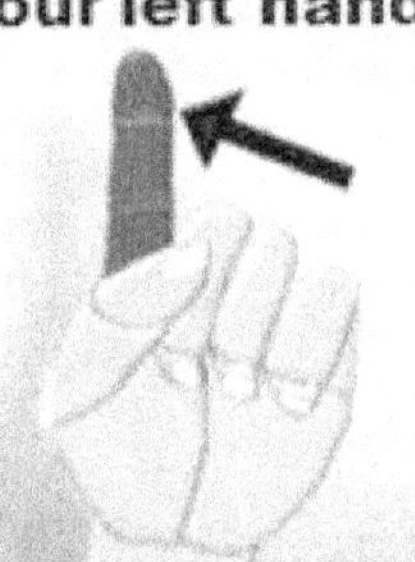

As you hold up the forefinger of your left hand, pray for them or it (if it is a situation). PRAY THEM UPWARDS. Wish them Agape Love and that all good things come their way. Whether or not you maintain a relationship with them, mentally send them on their way with your best wishes and blessings. Pray also they get their name written in the Lamb's Book of Life.

Pray the following prayer.

"Dear God, I release this person (or situation) to Your Holy Hands. I have forgiven them. I ask that You forgive that person as well. I wish only good things to come their way. I pray them upwards into Your Loving Arms. If it is your will, please write their name in the Lamb's Book of Life. That way, even if I never spend time with them again on this side of the veil, we will reunite in Heaven with only Agape Love between us. Once again, God, please forgive me for not forgiving them sooner. I thank You for being patient with my growth process. I pray this in Jesus' Holy Name. Amen."

"Heavenly Father, Holy Spirit, Lord Jesus, in Jesus' Holy Name, I pray that You share Your Divine Wisdom with me so that I know how to handle situations like this one in the future. I am so grateful that I have learned this vital lesson. I relish the opportunity to learn from You. I always want to operate according to Your Will and not my own. Please tell me what else you want me to know regarding this situation. I will be quiet now and listen for YOUR STILL SMALL VOICE. Thank you in advance for all you intend to teach me. Amen."

Then, LISTEN and INTUIT what the Lord wants you to know regarding this and similar situations.

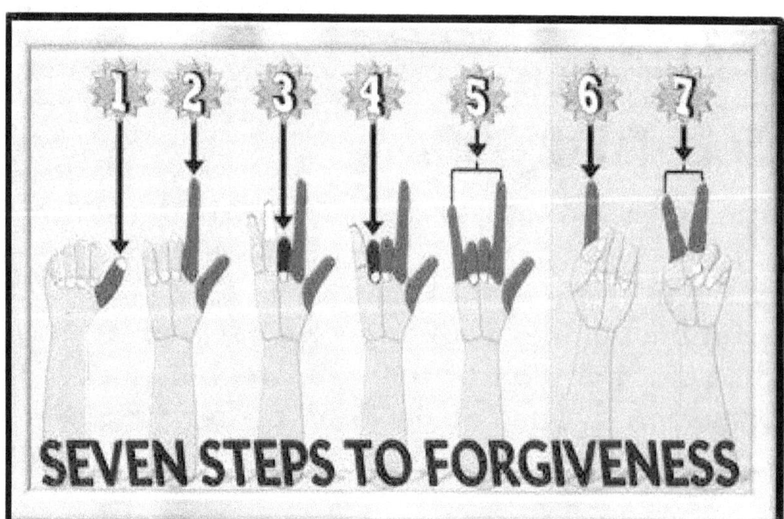

Forgiveness Is of paramount importance!

Even if you can't forget, you must forgive!

One of the many sins for which Jesus willingly sacrificed Himself on the cross was the sin of **REFUSING TO FORGIVE**.

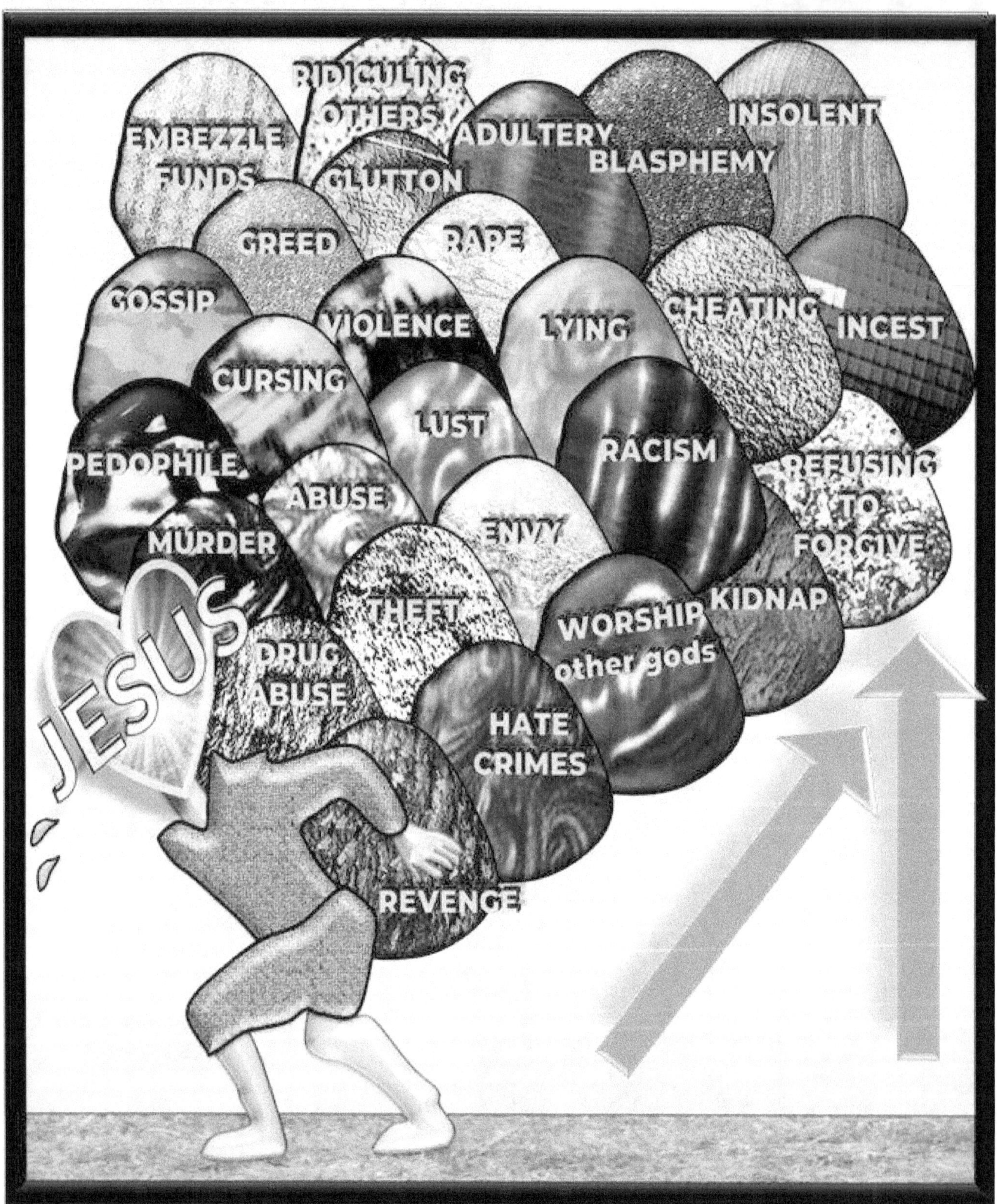

You are certainly allowed to be angry. In **Matthew 21:12-17**, **Mark 11:15-19**, **Luke 19:45-48**, and **John 2:13-16**, we learn that even Jesus felt righteous indignation when He witnessed greedy money changers turning His House of Worship into a dishonest marketplace. He knocked over their tables and forcefully drove them out of the Jerusalem Temple. Yet, our Lord did not sin. For example, Jesus did not follow them to their homes to take revenge. He would leave that determination in the hands of His Father in Heaven.

Observe what Paul wrote in the book of Romans about God's wrath.

Let's imagine that you live in a home where acts of Domestic Violence have taken place in the past or take place periodically even now. You have a perfect right to be angry. No man, woman, or child should have to be subjected to nor is deserving of acts of physical, emotional, psychological, or sexual harm.

If you are in **imminent danger**, here are **12 FREE resources** available for you and your children:

12 FREE resources available for you and your kids

1 Call **988** for the Suicide and Crisis Lifeline.

2 Call the National Domestic Violence Hotline at **800.799.SAFE (7233)** or **Text 88788**. They can extract you from the home and take you and your children to a Safe House.

3 If you have access to a computer, you can visit **safehouse.org** or call their Crisis Line at **(205) 669-7233 (SAFE)** or email **safehouse@safehouse.org**

4 In advance, arrange an odd word choice that you will text to a trusted loved one that you need them to call 9-1-1 on your behalf. For example, you might type '**peanut butter**' or '**peanut brittle**.'

5 Some women have been able to dial 9-1-1 and immediately say, "**I would like a pepperoni pizza delivered to _______ (and give your address)**." The dispatcher could then ask yes-no questions to determine if you cannot talk as someone dangerous is in the room. Otherwise, try to leave the phone on as long as possible so the dispatcher can try to locate you with latitude and longitude numbers and a ping from a nearby cell phone tower.

6 Some restaurants and bars have a notice inside the bathroom stalls of something you can pretend to order that will be a secret signal to the waiter, waitress, or bartender that will alert them that you need help.

7 If someone dangerous is trying to drive or walk you away, use this universal hand signal that will hopefully alert others to call **9-1-1**.

8 Find people you can trust to talk to, such as your church elders, family, relatives, friends, counselors, police, etc. If the first person you tell does not believe you, try somebody else. Keep trying until you find the right person to help and advise you.

9 The power of prayer can work wonders. "Faith Prayers hotline: Call 1-866-515-9406. Prayer and Hope prayer request hotline: Call **1-866-599-2264**. National Prayer Center Assemblies of God prayer line: Call **1-800-477-2937**. TBN Prayer Center: Call **714-731-1000** or visit their website to submit your prayer requests."

10 Jesus calls: **855-537-8722**. "How may I contact the Prayer Tower for prayers? You can call the Dallas Prayer Tower: US & North America **+1-855-537-8722 (or) 1-855-JESUS CALLS**. If in Canada, the Canada Prayer Tower: Canada **1-416-385-7677 or 1- 855-522-7729**. Call any time, day or night, for prayer support." It is FREE.

11 Call **1-800-329-0029** for the Daystar 24-hour prayer line.

12 Call **1-800-700-7000** for 700 Club Prayer Center.

You can focus on not forgetting but forgiving that person from a safe distance.

What might happen if you refuse to FORGIVE?

From that place of safety, it is vitally important to focus on forgiving that other person. There is no need to forget what they did, as you do not want to enable a repeat of that behavior should you decide to reconcile. Before you do, it would be a really wise idea to first take part in **solo and couple counseling**. If either or both of you are members of a church, temple, mosque, etc., it would be ideal to reach out to them for prayerful support.

Why must you forgive? Forgiveness is more about **keeping your communication lines open to Christ, our Heavenly Father, and the Holy Spirit**. If you muddy it up with grudge-holding, it will be hard to hear their voices. Also, consider these directives included in the Holy Bible:

> **Ephesians 4:26 "In your anger do not sin."** Do not let the sun go down while you are still angry, 27 and do not give the devil a foothold. (NIV)
>
> **2 Corinthians 5:10 For we must all appear before the judgment seat of Christ, so that each of us may receive what is due us for the things done while in the body, whether good or bad. (NIV)**

Remember, we are not guaranteed to wake up tomorrow morning. You might have a sudden health, weather-related, or other kind of crisis at night. Do you want to face the Triune God only to have to make excuses for why you were found still holding a grudge? As a thought experiment, this is how that conversation might go.

Recall the Bible story, from **Matthew 18:21-35**, called 'The Parable of the Unmerciful Servant'. In short, a servant owed more money than he could pay. In his benevolence, his master chose to erase the debt. But instead of paying that wonderful gift forward to others, the servant threw a fellow servant into the debtor's prison for being unable to pay back a much smaller sum owed to him. When the master finds out, he frees the one servant and throws his unmerciful servant into prison (aka hell). He would only allow him freedom once he had paid back his entire debt, even if it took the remainder of his life to do so.

In like manner, picture yourself standing in front of the Triune God: Father, Son, and Holy Spirit. First, they remind you that Jesus paid the debt for every sin you and everybody else ever committed. Next, Jesus asks, "Have you forgiven all the people who have sinned against you?"

14

You think back and recall you and your spouse discussed reconciliation.

Jesus smiled approvingly when you stated, "Given that I had vulnerable children, I did not feel it was in my or their best interests to live with him again; however, we were able to shake hands through a little window amicably. I kept a safe distance from him but still forgave him."

Jesus would also smile in approval if you stated, "Even though I did not feel it best to live with him again, he was always a wonderful dad to our kids. So, the two of us could amicably co-parent from our separate abodes. We were committed to not weaponizing our kids. In other words, we did not make demeaning comments about our former spouse to either of our kids."

On the other hand, you might feel forced to admit that you never could muster the strength to forgive your former spouse. You might even have been guilty of making demeaning comments about your former spouse loud enough for your kids to hear. Instead of an open line of communication, you self-righteously kept a brick wall between you.

I can't help wondering, even if you were saved and redeemed by the blood of Christ, would you barely squeak by and get into Heaven minus any or many rewards, or would you lose your Salvation and be sent to hell?

Judgment Day: Bema seat vs Great White Throne

This Google definition explains the difference between Christ's Bema Seat (or Judgment Seat) for BELIEVERS and the **Great White Throne Judgment Seat for UNBELIEVERS, Satan, and his fallen angels**. Only God knows the answer as to whether all Unbelievers go to hell who refused to accept Jesus as the Messiah. Perhaps Christ determines that verdict on a case-by-case situation based on other factors from their life.

> **Google quote**
>
> **Judgment Seat of Christ for Believers vs Great White Throne Judgment for Unbelievers**
>
> "What is the difference between the Judgement seat and the Great White Throne?
>
> It is where Satan, his fallen angels, and unbelievers are judged. It is the last judgment before all who oppose God are cast into the lake of fire. The Bema Seat of Christ, also known as the Judgment Seat of Christ, is where Jesus rewards Believers based on what they did to build His Kingdom."

Randy Kay, from Randy Kay Ministries (www.randykay.org), hosts a YouTube program about NDEs. Several years back, he died for over 30 minutes and saw Heaven. To explain why a sinful person could not be allowed into Heaven, he makes the analogy that this would be similar to a person who used a swimming pool like it was a toilet. The pool owner might need to drain the entire pool.

The Blood of Christ saves only believers.

As for the unbelievers, they will have to pay the debts for all the times they sinned (aka missed the mark). In other words, the CLOCK IS TICKING. Please choose Christ!

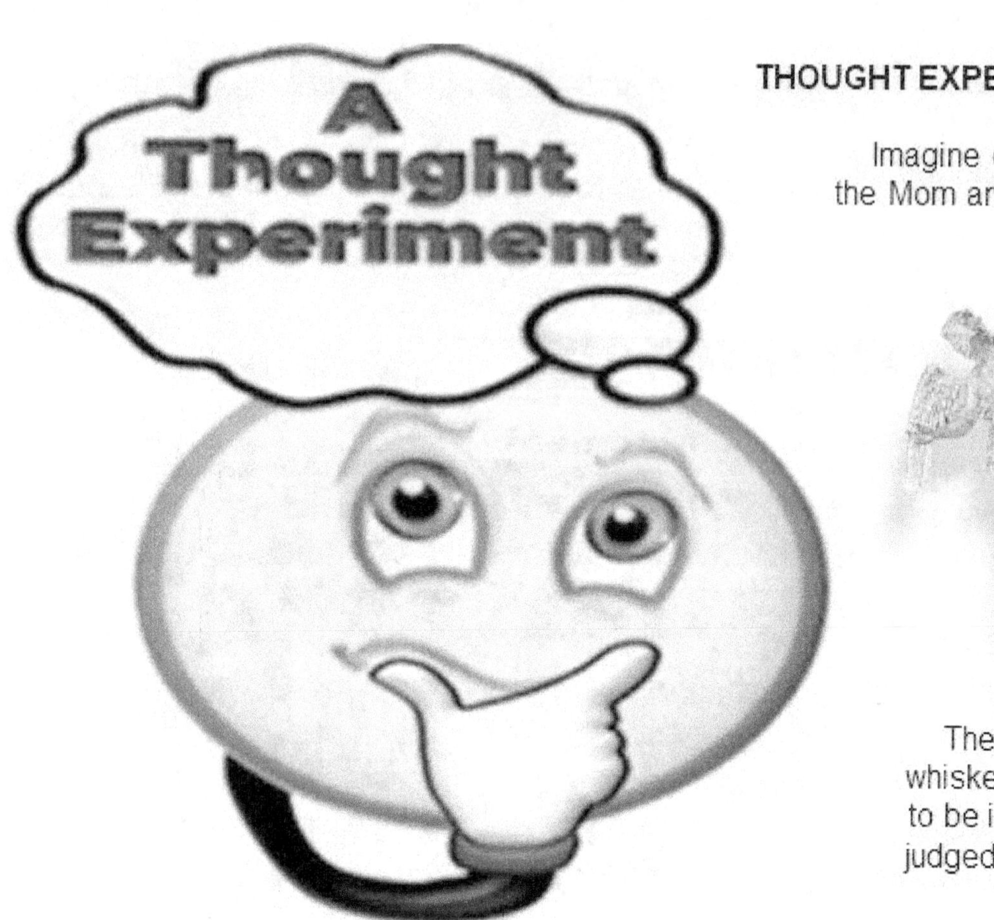

Imagine either or both
the Mom and the Dad died.

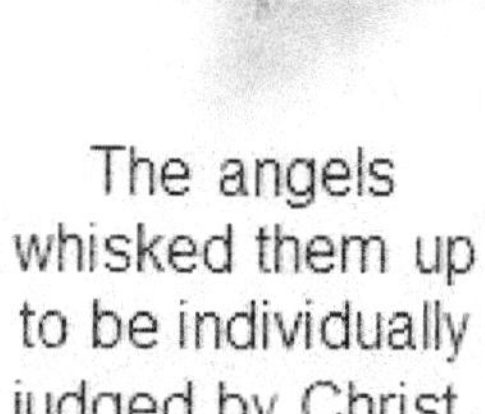

The angels
whisked them up
to be individually
judged by Christ.

God
No!
JESUS
HOLY SPIRIT
A Thought Experiment
Did you Forgive?
SCENE 1

God
No!
JESUS
HOLY SPIRIT
Did you Forgive?
SCENE 1
A Thought Experiment

Jesus asks the Mom, "**Did you FORGIVE?**"

With God the Father as a heavenly witness, if the woman says **NO**, Jesus will inform her, "**Therefore, since I can't FORGIVE you, I never knew you.**"

Source: Matthew 7:23

Jesus asks the Dad "**Did you FORGIVE?**"

With God the Father as a heavenly witness, if the man says **NO**, Jesus will inform him **"Therefore, since I can't FORGIVE you, I never knew you."**

Source: Matthew 7:23

THOUGHT EXPERIMENT for BELIEVERS: Here are two imaginary scenarios with two BELIEVERS facing judgment from Christ. I can picture them falling to their knees, overwhelmed by finally seeing King Jesus face-to-face. Wow! Just like that *Mercy Me* song, '*I can only imagine.*'

THOUGHT EXPERIMENT for BELIEVERS: Here are two imaginary scenarios with two BELIEVERS facing judgment from Christ. I can picture them falling to their knees, overwhelmed by finally seeing King Jesus face-to-face. Wow! Just like that *Mercy Me* song, '*I can only imagine.*'

Jesus invites each person to stand.

Jesus invites each person to stand.

Father God asks, "**How do you plead?**" Both confidently state, "**I plead the** BLOOD **of Jesus.**"

Father God asks, "**How do you plead?**" Both confidently state, "**I plead the BLOOD of Jesus.**"

Jesus opens the **Lamb's Book of Life**. Sure enough, He finds each of their names. So, He nods with approval and states, as seen in **Matthew 25:23**, "Well done, good and faithful servant." The Holy Spirit beams. Father God says, "**Welcome to Heaven!**"

God
JESUS
Well done, good and faithful servant!
HOLY SPIRIT
A Thought Experiment
SCENE 4

God
Well done, good and faithful servant!
JESUS
HOLY SPIRIT
A Thought Experiment
SCENE 4

Life Review for Believers

The next step is for each of them to witness their Life Review. From that, Jesus determines what rewards to offer. Here are some Bible verses that describe the five crowns that **BELIEVERS** might be able to earn.

Judgment Day: 5 Crowns earned by Believers

James 1:12 Blessed is the one who perseveres under trial because, having stood the test, that person will receive the **crown of life** that the Lord has promised to those who love him. (NIV)

1 Corinthians 9:25 And every man that striveth for the mastery is temperate in all things. Now they do it to obtain a corruptible crown; but we an incorruptible crown. (KJV)

2 Timothy 4:5 But you, keep your head in all situations, endure hardship, do the work of an evangelist, discharge all the duties of your ministry. 6 For I am already being poured out like a drink offering, and the time for my departure is near. 7 I have fought the good fight, I have finished the race, I have kept the faith. 8 Now there is in store for me the crown of righteousness, which the Lord, the righteous Judge, will award to me on that day—and not only to me, but also to all who have longed for his appearing. (NIV)

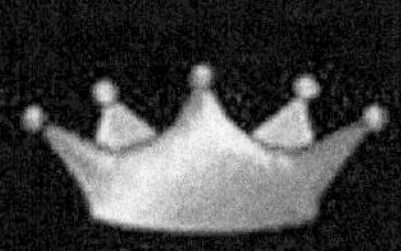

Crown of Glory

1 Peter 5:2 Be shepherds of God's flock that is under your care, watching over them—not because you must, but because you are willing, as God wants you to be; not pursuing dishonest gain, but eager to serve; 3 not lording it over those entrusted to you, but being examples to the flock. 4 And when the Chief Shepherd appears, you will receive the **crown of glory** that will never fade away. (NIV)

Crown of Rejoicing (aka Crown of Exultation)

1 Thessalonians 2:19 For what is our hope, our **joy**, or the **crown** in which we will glory in the presence of our Lord Jesus when he comes? Is it not you? 20 Indeed, you are our glory and **joy**. (NIV)

Philippians 4:1 Therefore, my brothers and sisters, you whom I love and long for, **my joy and crown**, stand firm in the Lord in this way, dear friends! (NIV)

As a final example, let's say you are struggling to come to terms with the verbal abuse you have received from your parents, your siblings, a relative, your significant other, your kids, a friend, an acquaintance, your boss, your co-workers, a teacher, an administrator, or a stranger. You might have received this in person, via text or phone call, on social media, or through cyberbullying.

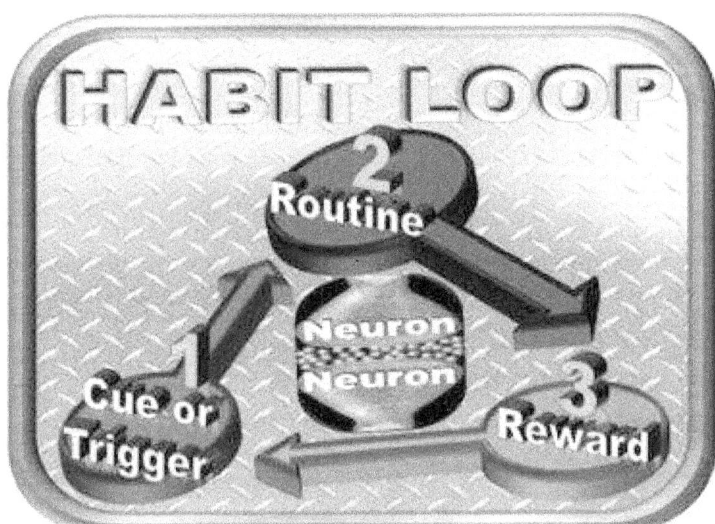

Perhaps this **CUE** or **TRIGGER** occurred due to a dream you had, sharing anecdotal memories with friends/loved ones, or someone began a sentence with "*Do you know what they said about you?*" You might have been reminded of this past name-calling when reading a book/story, watching a movie/video, listening to a podcast/radio show, or viewing a news story about someone taking revenge for something that happened in their past.

Before we discuss your habitual response to verbal abuse/name-calling, let's back up a moment. Our brain has hundreds of Neuron pairs whose only job is registering or reacting when a learned behavior, such as teeth-brushing, has become a habit. Your **CUE** or **TRIGGER** is that you register you have '*morning breath*' and perhaps a '*fuzzy-feeling film*' on your teeth. So, you head in the direction of the bathroom sink.

The very second you pick up your toothbrush or toothpaste tube, the neurotransmitters race to board that invisible train and start shooting off fireworks, so to speak, between the Neuron pairs that are part of their territory. Imagine this invisible train drives forward and backward between the Neurons until the habitual activity concludes.

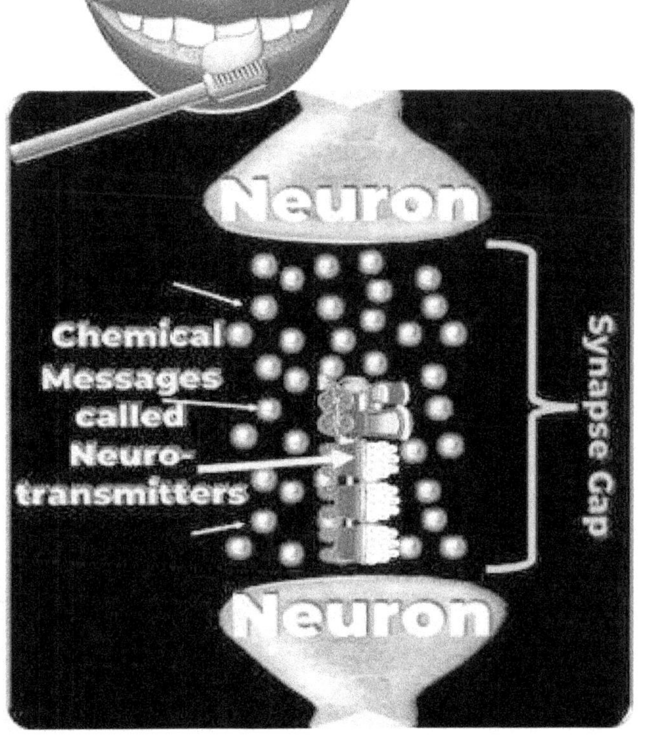

Since this is not a new habit, your brain has **CHUNKED** all the individual steps together so that you don't have to relearn all the steps that are part of that habit all over again. Now, you reference this activity as *'BRUSHING MY TEETH.'* As a child, you and your brain had to learn how to do each step:

- Pick up your toothbrush.
- Take the lid off the toothpaste tube.
- Squeeze the gel onto the brush bristles.
- Replace the lid.
- Slightly wet the gel on the brush.
- Stick the brush into your mouth and brush the front and back of your top and bottom teeth, the chewing surfaces of your teeth, gums, roof of your mouth, and tongue.
- Spit out the foamy mess into the sink.
- Rinse off your brush and place it in a toothbrush holder.
- Rinse out the inside of your mouth.

> ROUTINE: Brush teeth.
> REWARD: You have clean teeth and fresh breath.

Before you made this behavior a habit, the space between the Neuron pairs would look similar to this first illustration. Once toothbrushing became a habit, the space between the Neurons now looked like the second illustration.

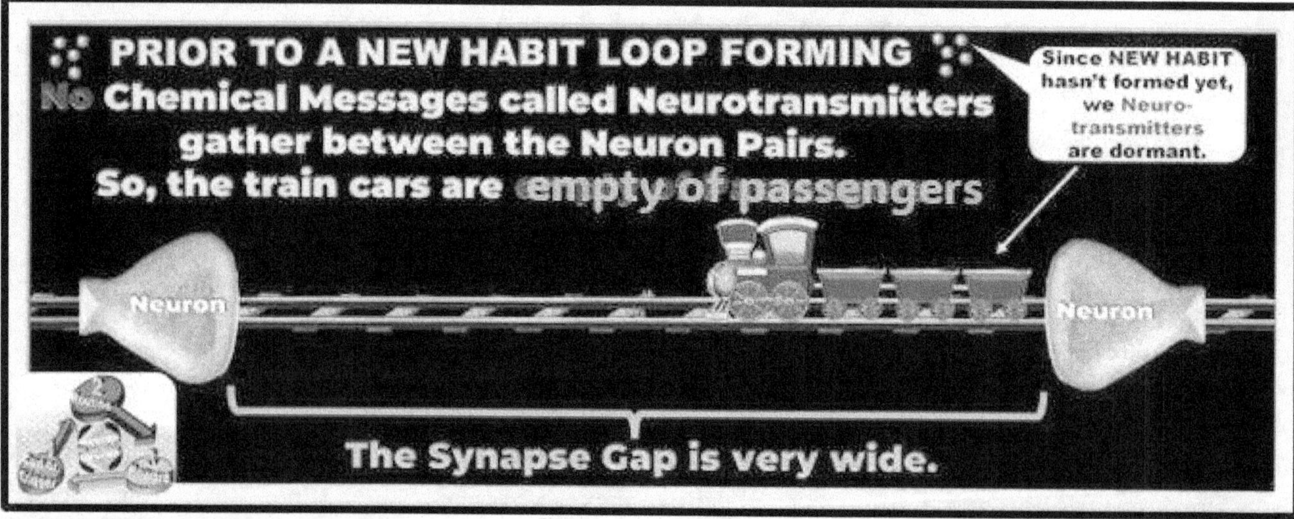

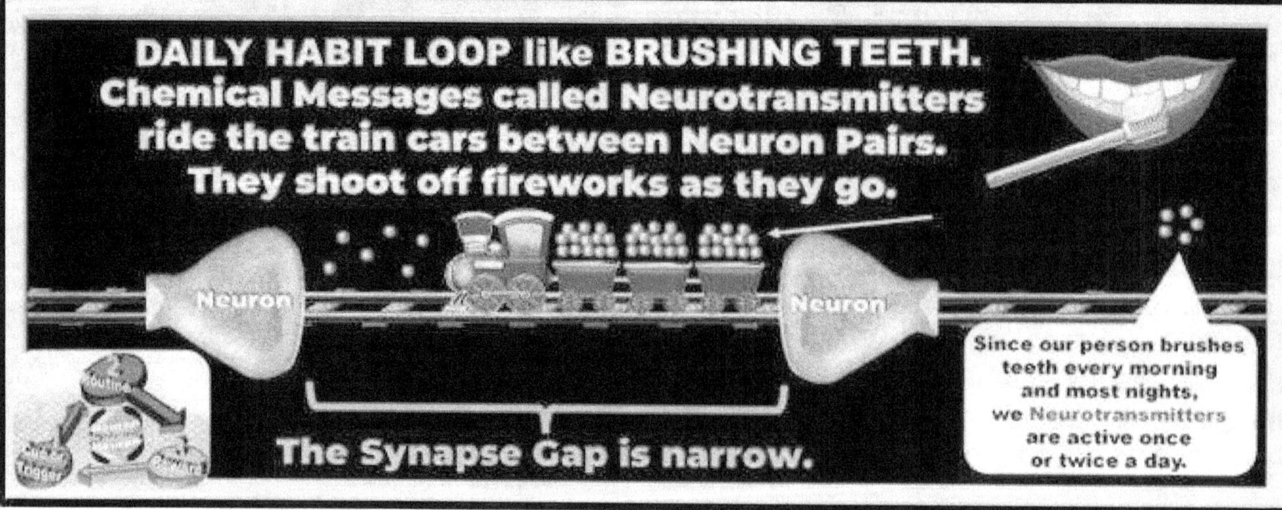

Another great example is driving a car. At one time, your brain had to register and learn each step involved. But now, picking up your car keys signals your neurotransmitters to start firing off each step into a cohesive whole called '*DRIVING YOUR CAR*.'

Because **brushing teeth** and **driving a car** are frequent habits, each neuron pair assigned to those tasks remains close together but never touches.

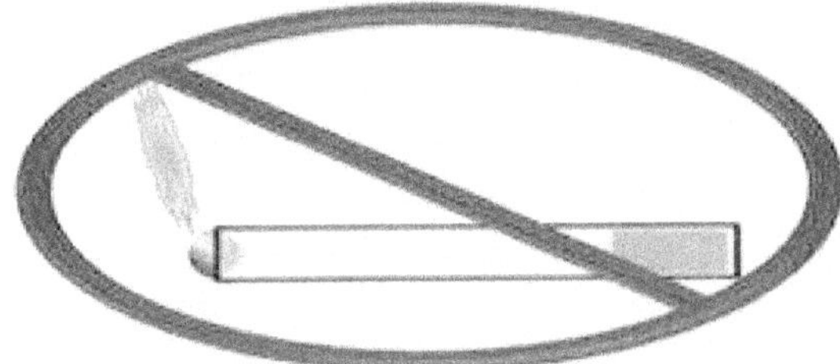

Let's imagine that you finally managed to quit smoking. Unfortunately, the Neuron pairs and neurotransmitters assigned to that past habit don't die or get assigned to a different habit. They drift further apart from each other and lie dormant in case they are needed again one day in the future.

But let's say you decided to light up a cigarette twelve years later. Immediately, the neurotransmitters would come out of retirement, activate, and begin firing between their assigned Neuron pair so that you can recall all the steps involved in the **CHUNKING** activity we think of as '*SMOKING A CIGARETTE*.'

FYI **Our clever brain Neurons are part of why HABITS are so challenging to break. To break a habit, you must de-CHUNK or change your learned ROUTINE (set of actions and reactions) to a more positive alternative.**

ATTITUDE

ROUTINE: You have to determine how to respond. There are only six options, as seen on the next page. You will receive either a positive or negative REWARD based on your choice. What will you do?

These are the Six Responses to Trauma: FIGHT, FLIGHT, FREEZE, FLOP, FRIEND (aka People Pleaser), plus Jesus. Which one is your Go-To?

For more info on each response, watch the 51-second YouTube video called The Five Fs: https://www.youtube.com/watch?v=H0be3LTETAk

YouTube Author:
Victim Support

Let's revisit the **SEVEN STEPS TO FORGIVENESS** process as you endeavor to forgive every instance of feeling verbally abused by name-calling. Consider journaling about this in a notebook to hold yourself accountable. Please recall that your sins are wiped out only to the extent that you have forgiven every person you feel has caused you harm in some way.

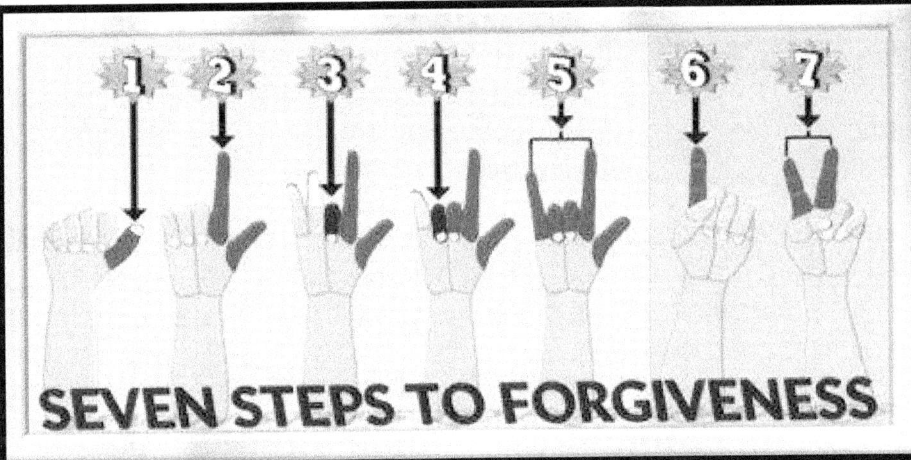

Recalling our THOUGHT EXPERIMENT for BELIEVERS in Jesus as our Lord and Savior, Father God asks, "How do you plead?" Both confidently state, "I plead the BLOOD of Jesus."

Jesus smiles and then frowns when He sees blots covering part of your name in His Lamb's Book of Life. He turns to Holy Spirit and asks, "Please, check to see if my BLOOD covers every part of his/her body." Holy Spirit checks. If FIGHT is your typical response to name-calling, He might see that there is no BLOOD covering your fist, your tongue you utilized to take verbal revenge on that person or through gossiping about them, or your feet you might have used to kick or trip that person. He might see no BLOOD covering your heart, head, or arm (if you are one who '*wears your heart on your sleeve*,' so to speak. Your heart quakes as you wonder what verdict He will render after watching your LIFE REVIEW. Please consider **FORGIVING** that person while you still have a chance. It would be sad if you lost out on some of your rewards. It would be tragic if God had to allow Satan to drag you away due to this technicality.

The previous scenario was a THOUGHT EXPERIMENT. Only the Triune God knows what will happen when you appear in front of Him on Judgment Day. If this is accurate, please take this exercise seriously. There are two reasons why I suspect it might happen just this way.

Reason 1: Some people who visited hell during an NDE reported they viewed multiple Christians in hell due to **REFUSING TO FORGIVE** others. A few NDErs said that 'Once saved, always saved' is a lie as they saw various Christians in hell due to being lukewarm, refusing to forgive, entertaining secret sins behind closed doors, being greedy and uncharitable to those in need, and not taking the Bible seriously. They even saw some Pastors there, as well, who espoused the 'Prosperity Church - Feel Good' view.

Reason 2: This is part of what Jesus preached during the **SERMON ON THE MOUNT**. I feel sure He didn't mean for you to actually cut off your hand or gouge out your eye. But very clearly, He painted the picture that you were in danger of being thrown into the Lake of Fire if you transgressed His laws.

> **Matthew 5:29** "If your right eye causes you to stumble, gouge it out and throw it away. It is better for you to lose one part of your body than for your whole body to be thrown into hell. **30** And if your right hand causes you to stumble, cut it off and throw it away. It is better for you to lose one part of your body than for your whole body to go into hell." **(NIV)**

Ezekiel 33:11 "**Say to them,** 'As surely as I live, declares the Sovereign Lord, I take no pleasure in the death of the wicked, but rather that they turn from their ways and live. Turn! Turn from your evil ways! Why will you die, people of Israel?'

Ezekiel 33:17 "**Yet your people say,** 'The way of the Lord is not just.' But it is their way that is not just. **18** If a righteous person turns from their righteousness and does evil, they will die for it. **19** And if a wicked person turns away from their wickedness and does what is just and right, they will live by doing so. **20** Yet you Israelites say, 'The way of the Lord is not just.' But I will judge each of you according to your own ways." **(NIV)**

As you begin with Step 1 of the 7-step forgiveness process, record every instance of **name-calling** where you suspect you might not have fully forgiven that person or group.

For example, as recently as my Christmas holiday in 2023, my younger brother and I recalled how when he was seven months old, in August of 1967, our dad was transferred from Kodak in Rochester, New York, to Tennessee Eastman Company in Kingsport, Tennessee. Several years apart, we both had the same elementary school teacher and voiced similar complaints about her. I also listed a couple of incidents that happened that year with fellow students that still bugged me.

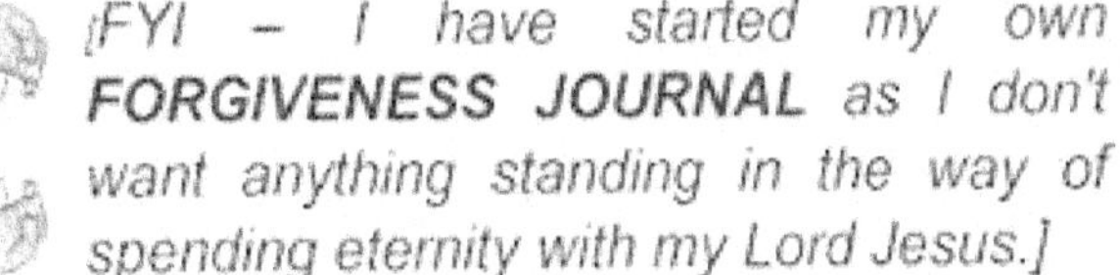

[FYI – I have started my own ***FORGIVENESS JOURNAL*** *as I don't want anything standing in the way of spending eternity with my Lord Jesus.]*

Since childhood triggers can still impact us as grown-ups, list those things. Then, analyze which of the six trauma responses you utilized when it happened and in the present time as you recall that event.

You might have chosen a **FIGHT RESPONSE** if you notice one of three things:
(1) You find yourself forming a fist.
(2) Your throat muscles tighten in readiness for making a verbal retaliation.
(3) A passive-aggressive form of this is when you spread gossip about that person to others.

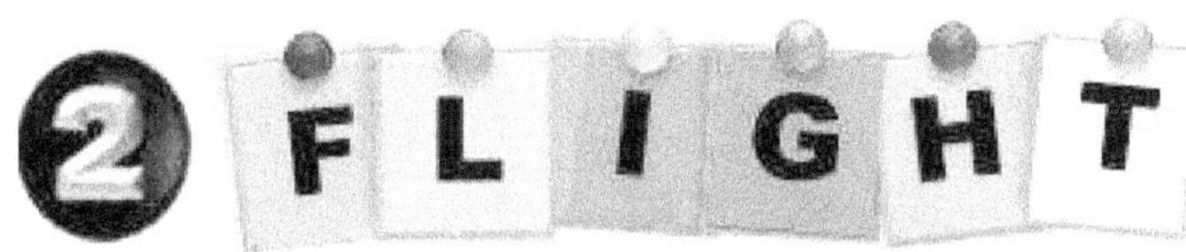

You might have chosen a **FLIGHT RESPONSE** if you notice one of two things:
(1) You ran off at the time, either crying, moping, or fuming. You might have even tattled to that kid's teacher or parents.
(2) You find yourselves making excuses about not feeling ready to deal with this issue, as what they did to you feels too overwhelming. There is no time like the present, as we are not guaranteed tomorrow.

Sometimes, we must also forgive others for hurting the people we love. Anger on their behalf is not healthy.

While growing up, my late husband experienced multiple instances of verbal and physical abuse by his earthly dad. Still, he kept making excuses about not having time to deal with his anger issues or the money to engage a counselor. Thank goodness for the altar call he made two weeks before dying from a massive heart attack. He finally was able to release all those pent-up negative emotions. He was in a state of euphoria for the final two weeks of his life. God took him home before he lost that emotional high.

 ③ FREEZE

You might have chosen a **FREEZE RESPONSE** if you notice one of two things:
(1) At the time, you froze in place, perhaps looking like a deer in headlights.
(2) This might be one of your issues if you still can picture how frozen and trapped you felt when this incident happened.

> *[I must admit that this is one of my GO-TO responses, as I don't do well with being screamed at. My journal is beginning to fill. What about you?]*

④ FLOP

You might have chosen a **FLOP RESPONSE** if you notice one of two things:
(1) At the time, you found yourself sighing a lot, pouting, whining, or retreating to your bedroom or a hideaway as you repeatedly recall how helpless and hopeless you felt.
(2) As you recall this time in your life, you find yourself leaning into that contagious feeling so that you might feel tempted to find things about your current life that make you feel similar emotions. Please be aware that this is the ENEMY, aka Satan, trying to steer you away from God.

⑤ FRIEND People-Pleaser FAWN

You might have chosen a **FRIEND (OR FAWN) RESPONSE, a form of PEOPLE-PLEASING,** if you notice one of three things:
(1) At the time, you found yourself striving to appease the perpetrator, not because you approved of them or their tactics but as the safest manner to survive this situation. Kidnap victims sometimes choose to do this as they hope this will motivate the kidnapper to be less vindictive.
(2) If you discover you tend to be a **PEOPLE-PLEASER**, this might be one of your GO-TO responses to trauma. A dear friend of mine was trained by her therapist to '**EXERCISE HER NO MUSCLE**.' Setting firm boundaries is essential to prevent people from exploiting your good nature.
(3) You pretend to be happy when you are suffering inside. If that is the case, find someone understanding to talk to. Also, prayer is always the best avenue for dealing with anything stress-provoking.

Choosing Jesus is always the correct response.

Take your journal list. Mine already has 15 events.

You can handle each incident individually or lump them together as you begin the 7-step process.

You might even add one line item that reads, "*All those things Holy Spirit knows I need to deal with that I cannot currently recall.*"

Step 1 of 7

Hold up your right thumb. The rest of the fingers are folded closed.

Ask forgiveness from God so He might, so to speak, give you the '*thumbs up*' gesture afterward.

Pray the following prayer.

"Dear God, I am so sorry that I have not yet forgiven all those people from today's journal list. I had no idea I had harbored so much unforgiveness in my heart. I may have to repeat this process every few days to ensure I have cleared out as many negative memories as possible. Holy Spirit, please continue to alert me to blockages within me requiring healing. God, please forgive me for not doing this sooner. I am so grateful for your patience and tolerance of me. I pray this in Jesus' holy name. Amen."

Focus this prayer on each person, group, or situation you have not yet fully forgiven.

Ephesians 4:32 Be kind and compassionate to one another, forgiving each other, just as in Christ God forgave you. (NIV)

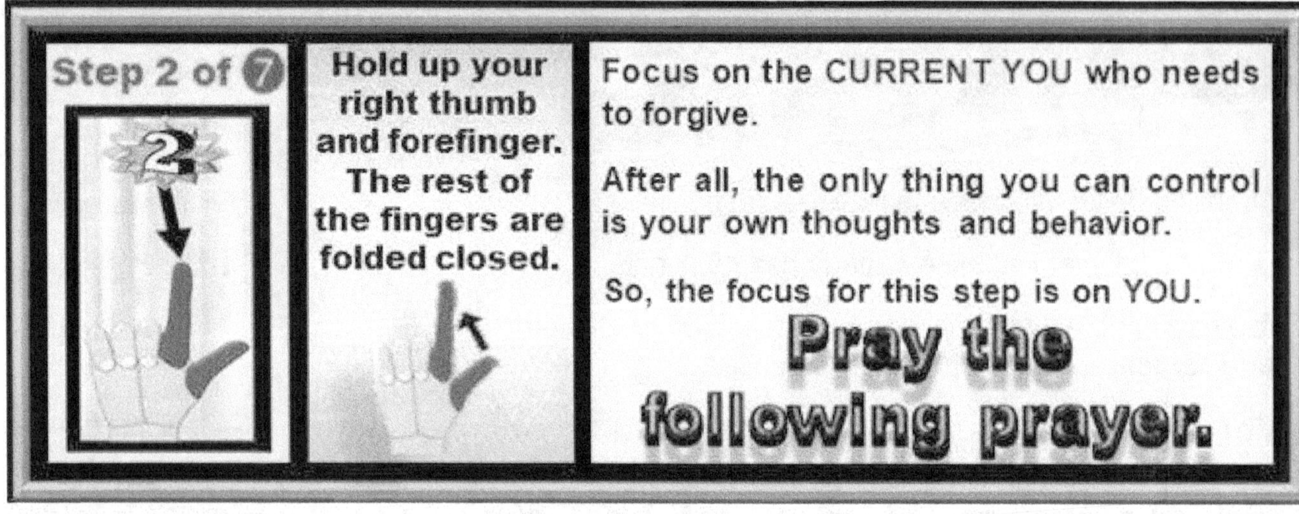

"Dear God, I am aware of Your directive in the Lord's Prayer that if I wish for You to forgive me, I must forgive others. Please give me the strength, moral courage, and ability to forgive this person, people, or situation(s) in Jesus' Holy name."

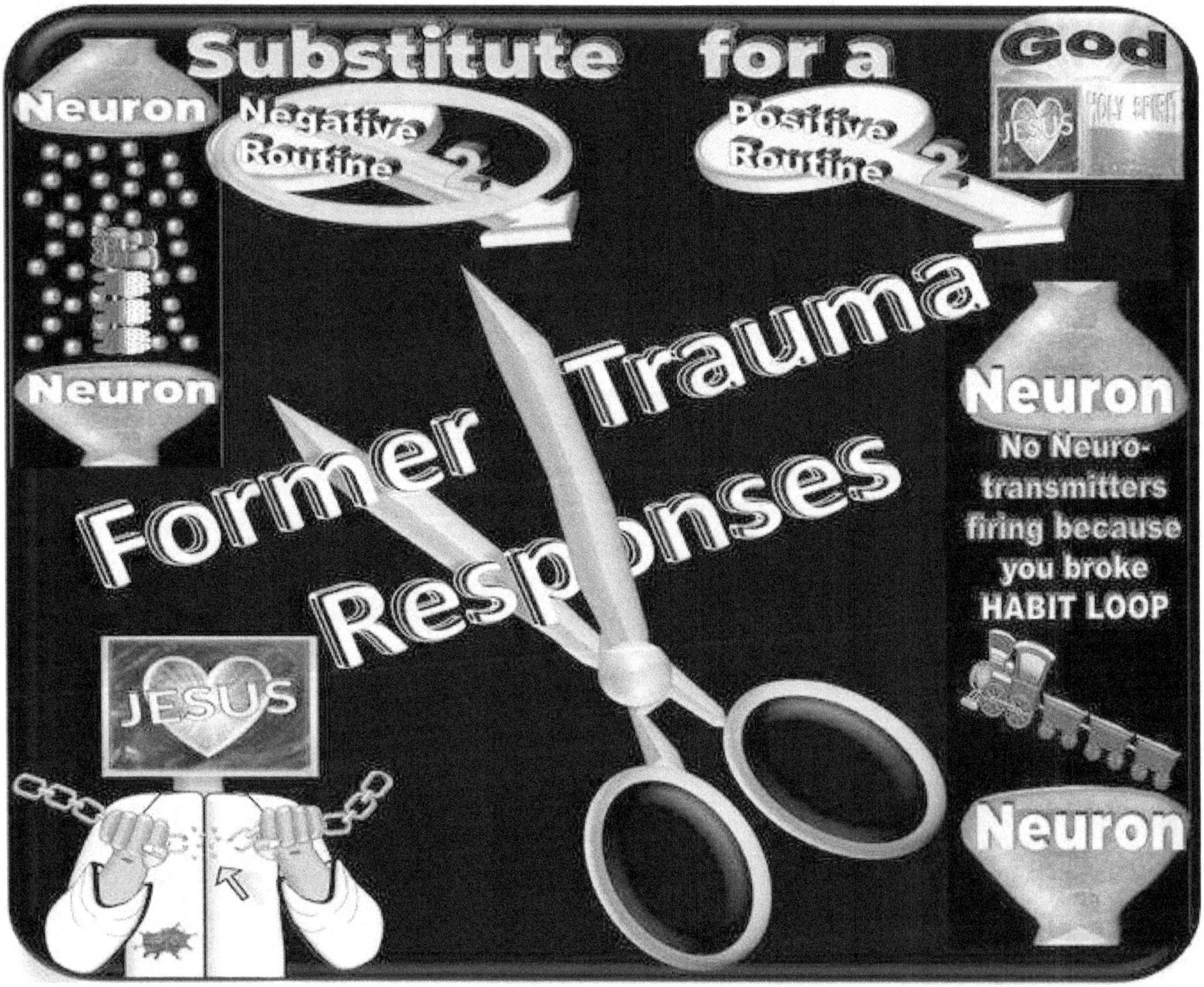

As you journal, consider having a heart-to-heart talk with the Neurotransmitters in your brain. Solicit their help to form a new **HABIT** that does not involve negativity. You might say something like, "Hey, Neurotransmitters. I know you were only trying to help when I reacted to name-calling with negative ROUTINES like FIGHT, FLIGHT, FREEZE, FLOP, FRIEND or FAWN (aka People-Pleasing). But as a Christian, I need to replace those old HABITS with new ones. I sure would appreciate your help to do that."

Heavenly Father, Holy Spirit, King Jesus, in Jesus' Holy name, please forgive me for my former negative responses to trauma. Please help retrain me and the Neurotransmitters in my brain to react in a more positive, loving, and forgiving fashion in the future.

S

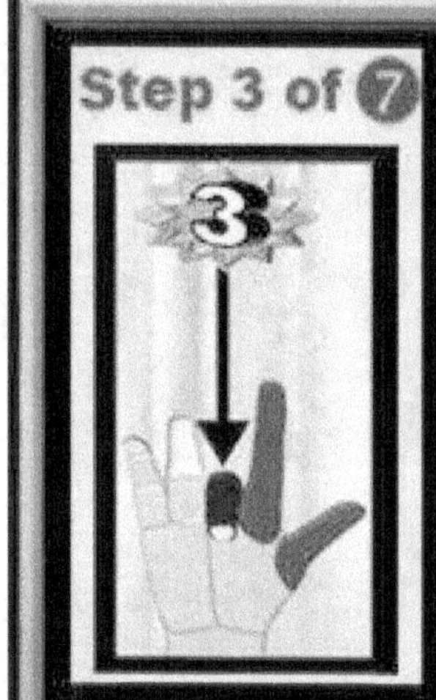

Hold up your right thumb and forefinger. Fold down your middle finger.

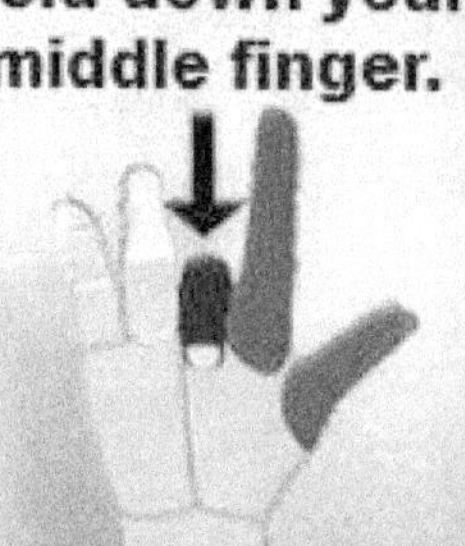

CURRENT YOU must forgive PAST YOU (whether it happened 5 minutes ago or 5 years ago, etc.) for not handling things as well as you could have.

"CURRENT ME forgives PAST ME for not handling things as well as I could have at that time. This is what I now understand (or realize)":

Hold up your right thumb and forefinger. Fold down your middle and ring fingers.

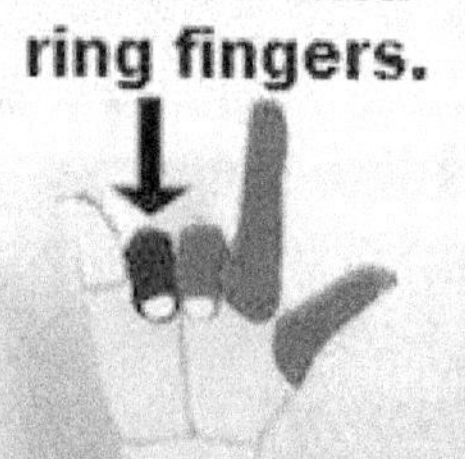

CURRENT YOU must forgive PAST THEM (or PAST IT if it is a situation).

"CURRENT ME forgives PAST THEM (or PAST IT if it is a situation). I forgive the person you were on that day. Knowing what we know now, we probably could have handled things better. This is what I now understand (or realize)":

Make the 'I LOVE YOU' sign language hand signal.

CURRENT YOU must forgive CURRENT THEM (or CURRENT IT if it is a situation).

With that 'I love you' hand signal, send Agape Love (Loving as Christ Loves, with a capital L) to that person or situation. **Pray the following prayer.**

"CURRENT ME forgives CURRENT THEM (or CURRENT IT if it is a situation). I forgive you and send you Agape Love (of Christ). I thank you for giving me this opportunity to learn some important lessons."

"Even though I no longer want you to be part of my life, I still wish all the best for you now and in the future."

"Also, I would like to communicate the following to you, in person or only in my thoughts: ____
____."

"I definitely want you to continue to be a part of my life. I wish all the best for you now and in your future."

"Also, I would like to communicate the following to you, in person or only in my thoughts: ____
____."

Suggestion: Look through your journal list. Consider putting an asterisk (*) by the names you still want to maintain relationships with.

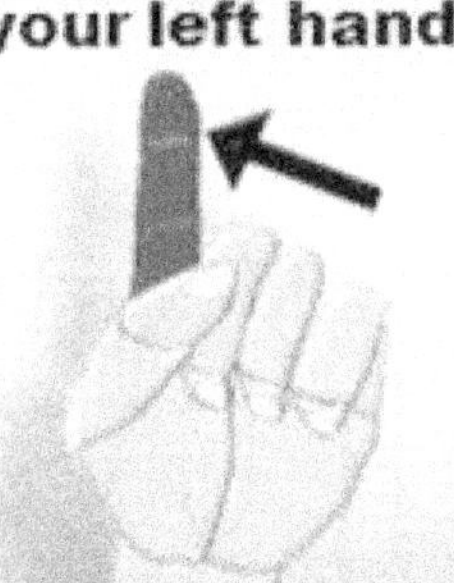

As you hold up the forefinger of your left hand, pray for them or it (if it is a situation). PRAY THEM UPWARDS. Wish them Agape Love and that all good things come their way. Whether or not you maintain a relationship with them, mentally send them on their way with your best wishes and blessings. Pray also they get their name written in the Lamb's Book of Life.

Pray the following prayer.

"Dear God, I release this person (or situation) to Your Holy Hands. I have forgiven them. I ask that You forgive that person as well. I wish only good things to come their way. I pray them upwards into Your Loving Arms. If it is your will, please write their name in the Lamb's Book of Life. That way, even if I never spend time with them again on this side of the veil, we will reunite in Heaven with only Agape Love between us. Once again, God, please forgive me for not forgiving them sooner. I thank You for being patient with my growth process. I pray this in Jesus' Holy Name. Amen."

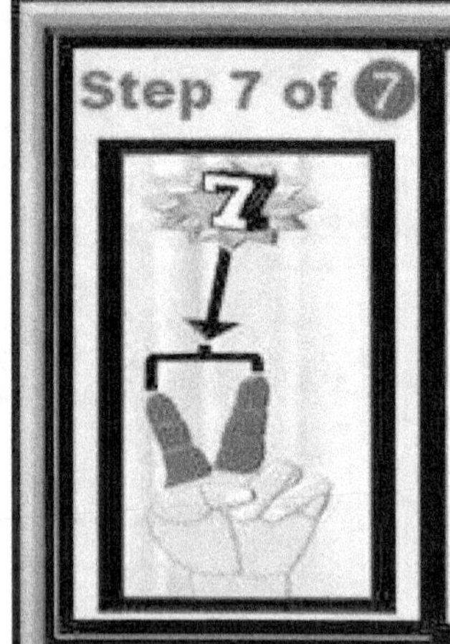

Make the 'peace' hand symbol with your left hand.

As you make the 'peace' hand signal with your left hand, ask God to teach you what else He would like you to learn from this situation. That way, you don't repeat the same mistake(s).

Pray the following prayer.

"Heavenly Father, Holy Spirit, Lord Jesus, in Jesus' Holy Name, I pray that You share Your Divine Wisdom with me so that I know how to handle situations like this one in the future. I am so grateful that I have learned this vital lesson. I relish the opportunity to learn from You. I always want to operate according to Your Will and not my own. Please tell me what else you want me to know regarding this situation. I will be quiet now and listen for YOUR STILL SMALL VOICE. Thank you in advance for all you intend to teach me. Amen."

Then, LISTEN and INTUIT what the Lord wants you to know regarding this and similar situations.

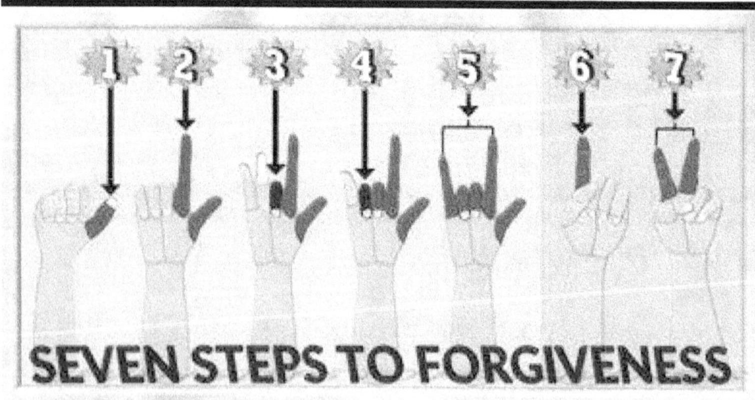

Desired Goal:

To conclude, look through your journal list. If you feel negative emotions when your eyes focus on a particular name, try working the 7-step forgiveness process and concentrate on just that one situation.

You'll know when you have successfully done this if you feel respectful upon seeing that person's name.

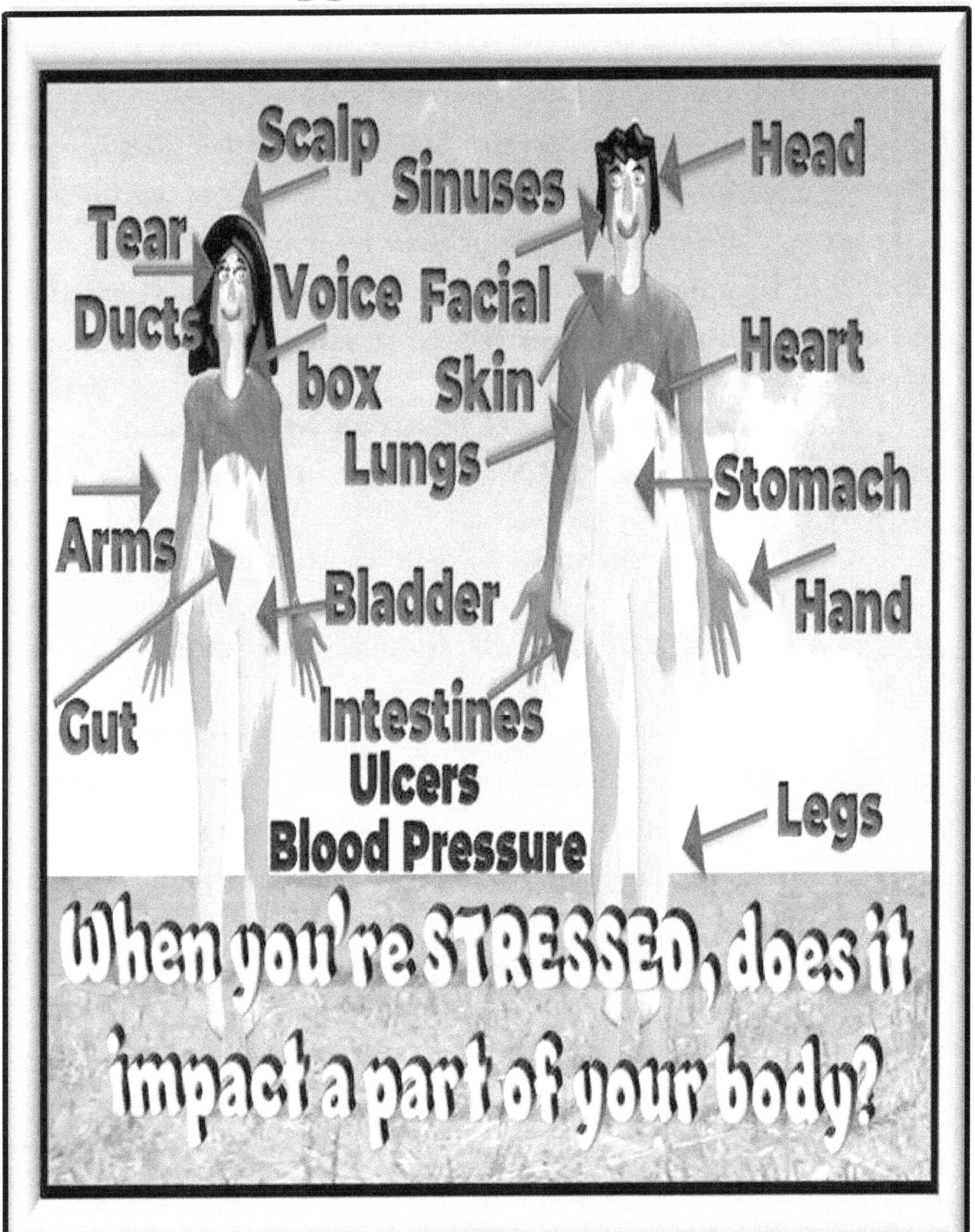

Scalp
Sinuses
Head
Tear
Ducts
Voice
box
Facial
Skin
Heart
Lungs
Stomach
Arms
Hand
Bladder
Gut
Intestines
Ulcers
Blood Pressure
Legs
When you're STRESSED, does it impact a part of your body?

Does stress impact a part of your body? Here are some examples:

- **Scalp** – Do the little hairs on your head feel electrified?
- **Head** – Do you get a headache or feel lightheaded or dizzy?
- **Tear Ducts** – Do you ever feel so angry you cry or get tearful?
- **Facial Skin** – Do stressful feelings seem to give you acne?
- **Sinuses** – Do your sinuses get activated when you feel stressed?
- **Voice Box** – Have you ever felt so stressed that you lost your voice?
- **Heart** – Does your heart ache or feel heavy when stressed?
- **Lungs** – Does stress make you short of breath or breathe erratically?
- **Stomach** – When stressed, do you comfort-eat or lose your appetite?
- **Gut** – Do you get strange gut feelings when stressed or feel bloated or odd?
- **Bladder** – Does your bladder get activated when feeling stressed?
- **Intestines** – Do you get intestinal issues when feeling stressed?
- **Hand** – Do you form a fist when feeling stressed or angry?
- **Arms & Legs** – Do your arms or legs feel like lead, tingly, numb, or frozen?
- **Ulcers & Blood Pressure** – Have you ever had these issues due to stress?
- **Other parts of the body** – Does stress impact some other parts of your body?

A famous quote by Aristotle: "Nature abhors a vacuum." Before concluding your FORGIVENESS process, ask the Holy Spirit to fill all the spaces in your body that might have formerly housed those grudges. That way, there is no room for any of Satan's minions to move in.

Luke 11:24 "When an impure spirit comes out of a person, it goes through arid places seeking rest and does not find it. Then it says, 'I will return to the house I left.' 25 When it arrives, it finds the house swept clean and put in order. 26 Then it goes and takes seven other spirits more wicked than itself, and they go in and live there. And the final condition of that person is worse than the first." (NIV)

Ephesians 6:10 Finally, be strong in the Lord and in his mighty power. (NIV) PRAYER

Ephesians 6:18 And pray in the Spirit on all occasions with all kinds of prayers and requests. With this in mind, be alert and always keep on praying for all the Lord's people. (NIV)

With the understanding that dis-ease (worry, anxiety) could transform into disease, you will be doing yourself a favor to get rid of all instances of grudge-holding, revenge, and hatred. Release all that to the Triune God and request the Holy Spirit to fill you with AGAPE LOVE, in Jesus' holy name. AMEN.

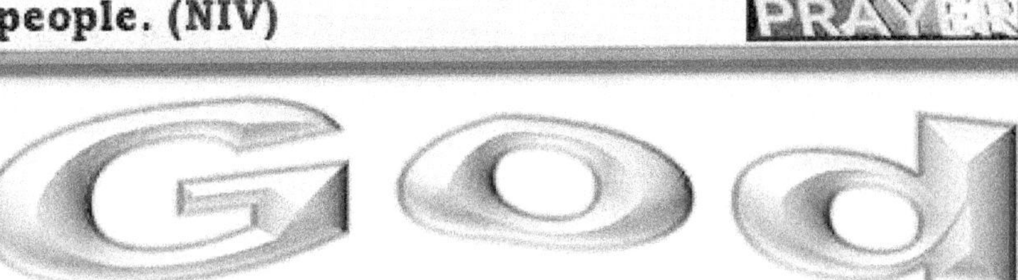

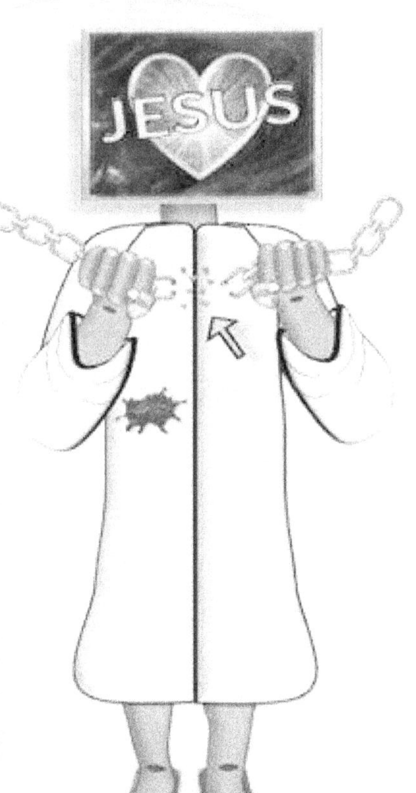

Philippians 4:6
Do not be anxious about anything, but in every situation, by prayer and petition, with thanksgiving, present your requests to God. 7 And the peace of God, which transcends all understanding, will guard your hearts and your minds in Christ Jesus. (NIV)

LORD'S PRAYER

Our Father, who art in Heaven.
Hallowed be Thy name.
Thy kingdom come.
Thy will be done,
on Earth as it is in Heaven.
Give us this day our daily bread.
Forgive us our trespasses
as we forgive those
who trespass against us.
Lead us not into temptation.
but deliver us from evil.
For thine is the kingdom,
and the power,
and the glory forever.
Amen.   Matthew 6:9-15, Luke 11:2-4

"Strive for
PROGRESS
NOT
PERFECTION"
--Author Unknown

PROGRESS
PERFECTION

Put on the **Armor of God** to protect you at all times. Read the Bible verses below to see more details about protecting yourself.

Ephesians 6:11 **Put on the full armor of God**, so that you can take your stand against the devil's schemes. 12 For our struggle is not against flesh and blood, but against the rulers, against the authorities, against the powers of this dark world and against the spiritual forces of evil in the heavenly realms. 13 Therefore put on the full armor of God, so that when the day of evil comes, you may be able to stand your ground, and after you have done everything, to stand. (NIV)

Years ago, I had a dream where I was driving up a steep hill. My car crested the hill. The setting sun had blinded my eyes to where I had to trust that there was a road on the other side of the steep hill instead of a drop-off. I woke up before I found out the outcome. I lay there and felt the Holy Spirit fill my being, reassuring me that there was nowhere I could go that God would not have me in His Loving sight. He told me, "God has laid a protective path of safety and well-being for you and for all of His beloved children)." That has been one of my mantras ever since.

Do you fear that if you let go of all your unforgiveness, especially the transgressions that may feel unforgivable, nothing of you will be left? The beauty is that if you let go of your grudges, you have much more space to house more of the Holy Spirit. That will be an incredible healing and blessing!

1. Describe your favorite Bible verse or verses demonstrating the vital need to forgive all others and all situations.

2. Journal about one of those situations as you work the seven-step finger signal process to explore whether you find this a helpful tool for learning to forgive others.

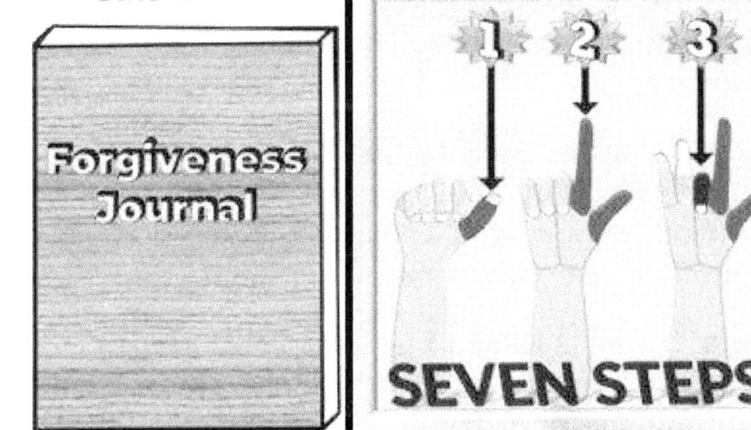

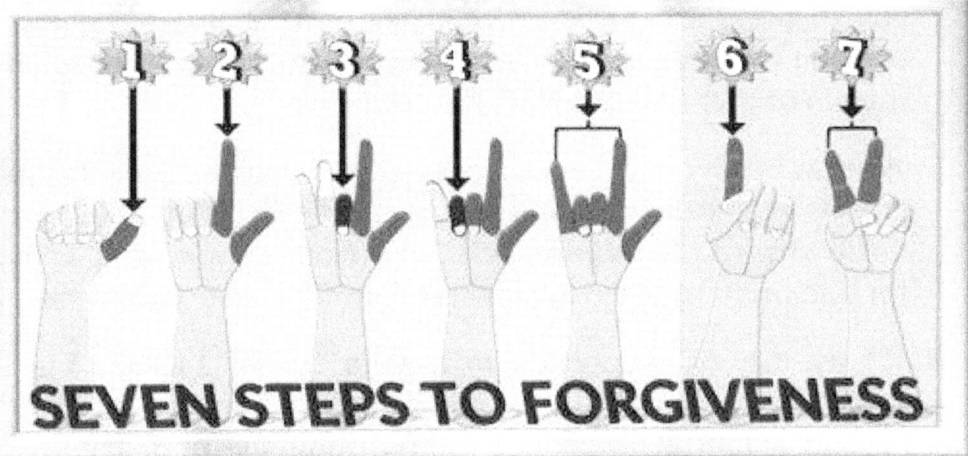

3. Examine the picture where Jesus is bearing sacks of multiple sins on His back. Think through your life. Journal about which of those sacks contains sins you might be guilty of. For example, one of those sacks includes the sin of CURSING. If you have ever used curse words in your life (inside your head or out loud to yourself or others), then you would add that sack to your list.

4. After you have completed that list, ask God for forgiveness for all the times you intentionally or unintentionally added to the heavy load of sins that Our Lord and Savior had to carry on the day of His crucifixion. Be comforted in knowing that as long as you truthfully list them, sincerely repent them, and ask for forgiveness, the Triune God forgives you in Jesus' Holy name. Thank God for that incredible gift!

5. Discuss or journal about the difference between WRATH versus RIGHTEOUS INDIGNATION. Give an example from your own life.

6. If you or someone you know is a victim of abuse, study the list of 12 suggested safety resources. You might want to implement #4 of using an odd code word to alert trusted others that you are in danger. You may also want to learn the "I'm in danger - call 9-1-1" hand signals and teach that signal to others. Study the list and make a note of any of them that might be useful to you or your loved ones.

7. What do you think will happen to you if you refuse to forgive other people's past or current transgressions against you? FYI - Remember, you do not have to forget these transgressions. Our Lord commands us to forgive. Imagine that you were ushered into Heaven today, tonight, or tomorrow. Like Paul, as described in 2 Corinthians 12:2-4, this visit may happen like a dream, an open vision, a near-death experience, or actual death. If you had to stand in front of Jesus, how would you respond if there is anyone you have a grudge against? If there is, get busy working on ways to forgive that person, group, or situation so that God will not lay the sin of UNFORGIVENESS at your feet.

8. All true believers in Jesus get to go to Heaven. Look at the description of the five crowns offered as rewards to some believers. Are you currently eligible for any of those crowns? If not, are there any changes you want to make to become eligible for one or more of those crowns? Journal your conclusions.

9. Study the six responses to trauma below: FIGHT, FLIGHT, FREEZE, FLOP, FRIEND, or TURNING TO JESUS. What is your go-to response when facing conflict or fearful situations? Journal about this or discuss this with others.

10. If your go-to response to conflict or fearful situations is any of the responses other than TURNING TO JESUS, what changes do you see yourself willing to take to change that? Journal about this or discuss this with others.

11. Start a FORGIVENESS JOURNAL so nothing stands in your way of spending eternity with our Lord Jesus. Attempt to recall people you may not realize you were still holding a grudge against. We must forgive all. We don't have to forget, but Jesus commanded us to forgive all people and situations.

12. Read through the list of parts of our body that are impacted when we feel stress. Make a list of the ones that apply to you. Then, ask the Holy Spirit to fill all the spaces in your body that might have formerly housed those grudges. That way, there is no room for any of Satan's minions to move in.

13. By reading through the Bible verses, Ephesians 6:11-13, journal about or discuss how you can put on the Armor of God to protect you from harm and the 'devil's schemes.'

14. As described on the road trip page, journal about or discuss Deuteronomy 31:8 about how God protects every step you take or plan to take. Journal about or discuss examples of how you have seen God protecting you from harm at various times throughout your life.

Author's Dedication

There are many ways to demonstrate our love for and worship of our Lord Jesus Christ. This book is a rendering of data points for you to prayerfully consider that might give your worship of Him a deeper dimension. I dedicate this book to all honest seekers of truth. May it provide another viewing point of the **WORD** in the Holy Bible.

Author's Acknowledgements

There was a deeper purpose for authoring this book. I wrote this book not for my glory but for the glory of our Heavenly God the Father, God the Son, and God the Holy Spirit. I am so grateful for all the manifold ways God, the **Trinity of three Persons**, continually blesses my life. May this book bless your life, as well.

I acknowledge and am so grateful for all the people who created the Bible APPS, Google, Microsoft PowerPoint, Microsoft Word, the Paint APP, books, videos, movies, talks, and sermons that fed my imagination and blessed my life. I also acknowledge the countless moments of comfort and blessings I receive from my dear and treasured family and friends (both living and deceased), of which I count you, my readers, among them. I am eternally grateful! God bless you all! May you have a blessed and touched-by-God life!

Final Blessings

I find myself speculating if God planted me exactly where He did and gave me all the experiences that He gave me just so I could write this book.

And then I feel the **Holy Spirit** nudging me, reminding me of this Bible verse:

Romans 8:28 And we know that all things work together for good to them that love God, to them who are called according to his purpose. (KJV)

May the **Holy Spirit** touch and bless you, as well, and help you to fulfill the mission that God has prescribed just for you.

I end this book with two final blessings, one by King David, the other by Moses.

Psalm 121:8 The Lord keeps watch over you as you come and go, both now and forever. (NLT)

Numbers 6:24 The LORD bless you and keep you. 25 The LORD make his face shine upon you and be gracious to you. 26 The LORD turn his face toward you and give you peace. (NIV)

AMEN. Thank you for making the time to read a part or all of this book. Kindly consider leaving a review, even if it is only a sentence or two.

Also, if you found it pleasing, please share this book with the people you love.

BIBLIOGRAPHY

Bibliography: Used for entire book

Bible Gateway.com. (October 2023 to April 2024). Read the Bible. Website;
https://www.biblegateway.com/

Developer Unknown. (October 2023 to April 2024). Bible – Daily Bible Verse KJV. From a free cell
phone APP.

Google.com Search Engine. (October 2023 to April 2024).

Grammarly.com for editing (October 2023 to April 2024).

Kairos Software LLC. Developer. (October 2023 to April 2024). Bible KJV Strong's Concordance.
From a free cell phone APP. (October – November 2023)

On-line dictionary via Google Search Engine. (October 2023 to April 2024).

Bibliography: Resources to increase my understanding

Brain Facts.org. (December 2023). How Many Neurons Are in the Brain? Website:
https://www.brainfacts.org/in-the-lab/meet-the-researcher/2018/how-many-neurons-are-in-the-
brain-120418

Brownell, Dan. (November 2023). Jesus in the Old Testament. Website:
https://pointmetojesus.com/jesus-in-the-old-testament/

Deep Believer on YouTube. (October 2023 to April 2024). Videos about Near Death Experiences, Etc.
Website: https://www.youtube.com/@DeepBelievers/videos

Kay, Randy for Randy Kay Ministries on YouTube. (October 2023 to April 2024). Videos about Near
Death Experiences, etc. Website: https://www.youtube.com/@RandyKayMinistries/videos

New World Encyclopedia. (December 2023). Corrie ten Boom. Website:
https://www.newworldencyclopedia.org/entry/Corrie_ten_Boom

Ramgopal and Arte for Presentation Process. (November 2023). How To Create Beautiful Chain
Graphic in PowerPoint. Website: https://www.youtube.com/watch?v=jjioPJ-_gIk

Ramgopal and Arte for Presentation Process. (October 2023). How to Create Clock Needle Animation
Effect in PowerPoint. Produced by Presentation Process. Website:
https://www.youtube.com/watch?v=3XVrJnFok88&t=267s

Ramgopal and Arte for Presentation Process. (November 2023). How to create Jigsawed Puzzle from
Picture in PowerPoint. Website: https://www.youtube.com/watch?v=b-WZjv5Xglc&t=491s

Roth, Sid for Sid Roth's It's Supernatural on YouTube. (October 2023 to April 2024). Videos about
Near Death Experiences, etc. Website: https://www.youtube.com/@sidroth/videos

The Bible Nerds. (December 2023). Remez: A Hint For Better Bible Study. Website:
https://thebiblenerds.com/remez-a-hint-for-better-bible-study/

Touching the Afterlife on YouTube. (October 2023 to April 2024). Videos about Near Death
Experiences, Etc. Website: https://www.youtube.com/@TouchingTheAfterlife/videos

Turner, Pastor Eddie. (October 2023). Revelation Wk. 1 from LIVELIFE.Church on YouTube. Website:
https://www.youtube.com/watch?v=5m9x6Lmdz0I&t=1s

Victim Support on YouTube - 51 seconds long. (December 2023). The Five Fs. Website:
https://www.youtube.com/watch?v=H0be3LTETAk

Wikipedia.org. (March 2024). Matthew the Apostle. Website:
https://en.wikipedia.org/wiki/Matthew_the_Apostle

On the following 4 pages, you will find 12 Free Safety Resources for you and your kids

Please note that you can photocopy those 4 pages, keep them in your pocket or purse, and share them with those in need.

Psalm 121:8 The Lord keeps watch over you as you come and go, both now and forever. (NLT)

12 Free Safety Resources for you and your kids

Observe what Paul wrote in the book of Romans about God's wrath.

Let's imagine that you live in a home where acts of Domestic Violence have taken place in the past or take place periodically even now. You have a perfect right to be angry. No man, woman, or child should have to be subjected to nor is deserving of acts of physical, emotional, psychological, or sexual harm.

If you are in **imminent danger**, here are **12 FREE resources** available for you and your children:

12 FREE resources available for you and your kids

1 Call **988** for the Suicide and Crisis Lifeline.

2 Call the National Domestic Violence Hotline at **800.799.SAFE (7233)** or **Text 88788**. They can extract you from the home and take you and your children to a Safe House.

3 If you have access to a computer, you can visit **safehouse.org** or call their Crisis Line at **(205) 669-7233 (SAFE)** or email **safehouse@safehouse.org**

4 In advance, arrange an odd word choice that you will text to a trusted loved one that you need them to call **9-1-1** on your behalf. For example, you might type **'peanut butter'** or **'peanut brittle.'**

Text odd phrase: Peanut Brittle

(**5**) Some women have been able to dial **9-1-1** and immediately say, "I would like a pepperoni pizza delivered to _______ (and give your address)". The dispatcher could then ask yes-no questions to determine if you cannot talk as someone dangerous is in the room. Otherwise, try to leave the phone on as long as possible so the dispatcher can try to locate you with latitude and longitude numbers and a ping from a nearby cell phone tower.

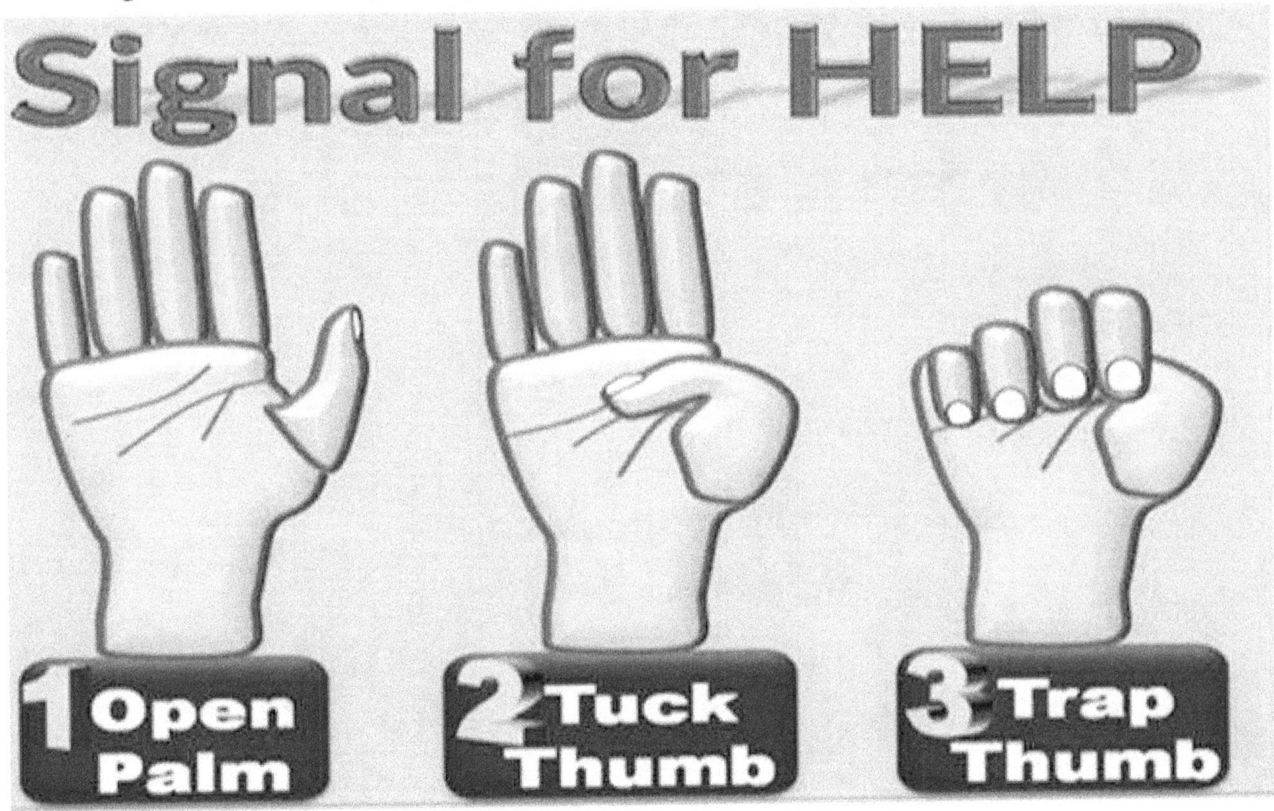

(**6**) Some restaurants and bars have a notice inside the bathroom stalls of something you can pretend to order that will be a secret signal to the waiter, waitress, or bartender that will alert them that you need help.

(**7**) If someone dangerous is trying to drive or walk you away, use this universal hand signal that will hopefully alert others to call **9-1-1**.

(8) Find people you can trust to talk to, such as your church elders, family, relatives, friends, counselors, police, etc. If the first person you tell does not believe you, try somebody else. Keep trying until you find the right person to help and advise you.

(9) The power of prayer can work wonders. "Faith Prayers hotline: Call **1-866-515-9406**. Prayer and Hope prayer request hotline: Call **1-866-599-2264**. National Prayer Center Assemblies of God prayer line: Call **1-800-477-2937**. TBN Prayer Center: Call **714-731-1000** or visit their website to submit your prayer requests."

(10) Jesus calls: **855-537-8722**. "How may I contact the Prayer Tower for prayers? You can call the Dallas Prayer Tower: US & North America **+1-855-537-8722 (or) 1-855-JESUS CALLS**. If in Canada, the Canada Prayer Tower: Canada **1-416-385-7677 or 1- 855-522-7729**. Call any time, day or night, for prayer support." It is FREE.

(11) Call **1-800-329-0029** for the Daystar 24-hour prayer line.

(12) Call **1-800-700-7000** for 700 Club Prayer Center.

You can focus on not forgetting but forgiving that person from a safe distance.